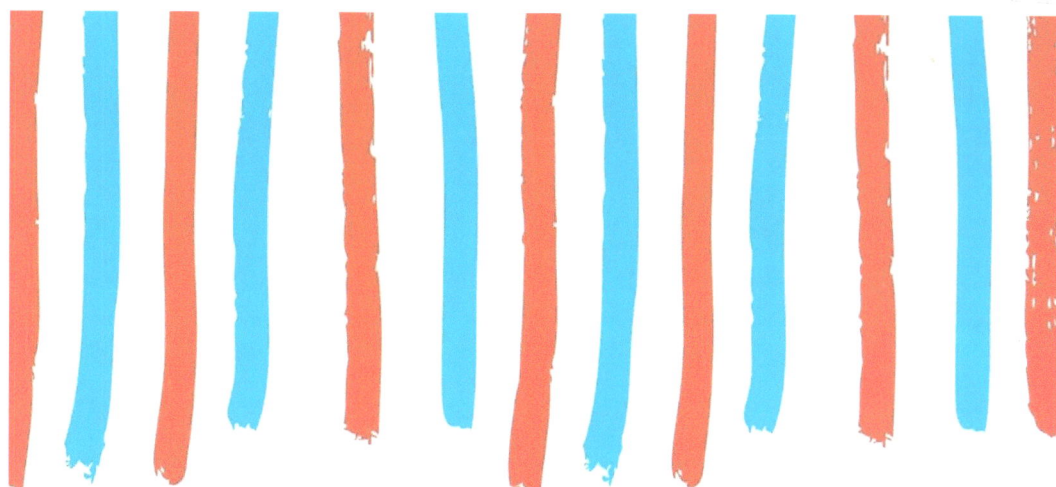

28 Best Games & Songs For Early Childhood Gym

BY CAMERON EDELMAN

28 Best Games & Songs
For
Early Childhood Gym

Cameron Edelman

Absolute Author
Publishing House

28 Best Games & Songs for Early Childhood Gym
Copyright 2019
Cameron Edelman

Publisher: Absolute Author Publishing House

Editor: Dr. Melissa Caudle

Library of Congress Cataloging-in-Publication Data

Edelman, Cameron

     28 Best Games & Songs for Early Childhood Gym/Cameron Edelman

        p. cm.

  ISBN: 978-1-951028-03-9

1. Education   2. Childhood Education   3. Health and Recreation

WHAT'S INSIDE

28 Best Games & Songs for Early Childhood Gym includes...

    ✓ **14** of the best games and activities for children ages three to six years

    ✓ **14** of the best songs that engage children ages three to six years and a link to the playlist.

    ✓ **28** Best tips, tricks, and things to remember when teaching Early Childhood.

Table of Contents

Preface

Well, it starts like this, a part-time job teaching sports classes, only to find out on the first day the sports classes are few and far between. Your main job will be teaching early childhood creative movement classes, which was something I had not done before, so I was confident in my ability to connect with children and think on my feet. That first day on the job and for the subsequent next few weeks, I was supposed to shadow the current early childhood gym teacher. The only problem with this plan was that they were not very good at their job. So, knowing truly little about teaching creative movement early childhood classes to three to six-year-olds, I took over the classes on that first day and never looked back. After spending hours scouring the internet to find anything I could on teaching early childhood, I located games and activities that were age appropriate for this age group.

Let me tell you it was not easy finding that information, but I discovered enough ideas to get started. Using my creativity and natural ability to work with children, I learned rather quickly what worked and what did not work. I am only gloating, which I won't do in the whole book I promise!

During those first few weeks, I put together lesson plans and found out what games and activities were a hit with the children and which ones I probably should not try again. I learned to quickly change things up if a game was not working and how to keep the children engaged and in no time; I loved my gig as a part-time early childhood gym teacher. That was seven years ago, and I really cannot believe how far I have come.

If I was having a bad day, teaching was always something that lifted my spirits seeing how excited the kids were to see me put the biggest smile on my face and I owed it to them to give them my best and most energetic self every class. These past seven years took me from never working with early childhood to helping write the gym curriculum for multiple early childhood sites to teaching at multiple preschools and getting to share my passion for working with early childhood with so many! However, the one thing I always go back to was how hard it was to find excellent early childhood gym curriculum.

The good news was that it forced me to be creative and come up with my own creative games and activities. It also made me wonder what everyone else was doing to create curriculum and realized there was a real need for early childhood gym curriculum. After many years of thinking about authoring a book to help out my fellow early childhood gym teachers, summer camp counselors and parents, I finally did it, and here it is! Please enjoy and share these games, songs, and fun with teachers and children alike.

1. Bear in the Cave

How to Play Bear in the Cave

Equipment Needed

- 8 Cones
- 2 Nets

Set-Up

Place two soccer nets on opposite sides of boundaries to use as the bear caves.

Create a circle in the center out of cones and have children sit in it. This is the force field that bears cannot go in. The force field is the cabin they found in the woods, and children are safe inside of there.

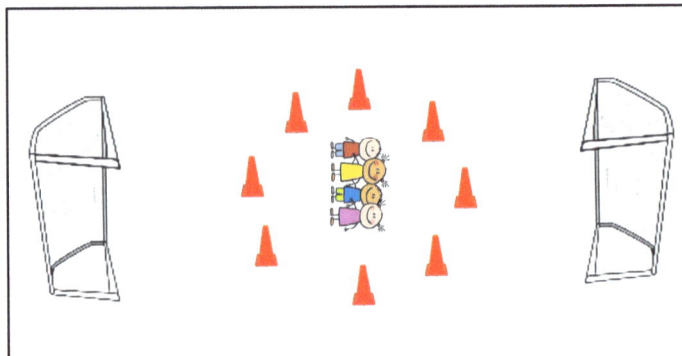

Instructions

1. Explain to children that instructor, that's you, led them the wrong way in the forest, and now they are lost and stumbled upon a cabin (the circle of cones).
2. They are safe in the cabin from the instructor who plays the role of the bear and tries to run into the cabin. However, you fall and get zapped when you try. When you do, it will get a laugh out of the children and get them engaged, so it is important that you fall.
3. When you say, "Running lost hikers," children must leave the cabin and run around the gym in the same direction to avoid injury. Let the children know the bear cannot get them; yet, so they can run around without getting tagged.
4. When you yell, "Bear, bear, bear," that's when the children must get to a net, which is the cave, within ten seconds as fast as they can without getting tagged.
5. If the children are tagged, they must freeze and need to be unfrozen by a friend. To keep the children engaged, try not to tag them the first round; just make it look like you are trying too.
6. Once they are in the cave, you can pretend they are eating your food and say to them, "Are you in my cave eating my grapes," and they will, in response need to say, "Yes." This dialogue will also keep them engaged and having fun.
7. Next, tell them you are going to wait outside the cave all night, so they don't escape, but you will fall asleep, snore, and at that time the children must tiptoe back to their cabin without waking the bear up.
8. Repeat one or two more rounds!

Variations

- Play multiple rounds, e.g., first round they run, next round they gallop, and third round they jump.
- Can be used with sports equipment as they run. For example, they can dribble a soccer ball or basketball around the gym before you say, "Bear, bear, bear."
- If they get tagged, they can have a choice to join you as a bear or stay as a lost hiker. Giving them an opportunity to choose will help them with decision-making skills, and there will be fewer tears!

2. Smash the Cheese

Equipment Needed

- 1 cheese wedge or gym mat
- 1 Poly Spot

Set-Up

Have children sit against the wall or wherever the boundary line is established.

Place one poly spot in front of the children.

Ten Yards away from the poly spot, place the cheese wedge up on its edge with the tip pointed toward the sky.

Choose the first child and ask them to stand on the poly spot with both feet.

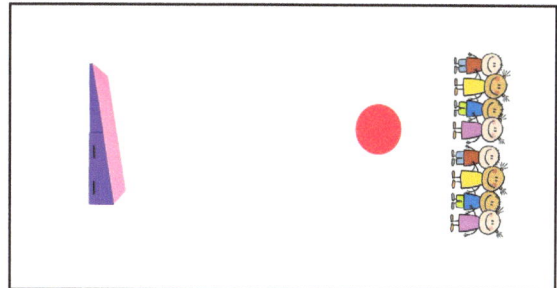

Instructions

1. One child will go at a time. The first child will start with both feet on the poly spot.
2. The instructor will stand to the side of the cheese wedge that is standing up on its edge.
3. The instructor will yell, "One, two, three, smash that cheese."
4. The child will then run toward the cheese wedge and jump into it belly first with their hands up and try to knock it over. When the child jumps into the cheese wedge, their momentum will knock it down.
5. Then the child is to run down the cheese wedge and sit down in a designated area on the other side of the wedge.
6. Each child is to get a turn.
7. Have the children who have already gone sit on the other side of the cheese wedge about five yards from where it will land when knocked down. The children will get a fun breeze that will blow their hair all over. It will keep them entertained and engaged after their turn is over.

Variations

- Play smash the coach. In this version, not only do they get to knock the cheese over but also the coach who will be walking across. The children have to time their run and jump so that the coach gets trapped under the cheese wedge, which is a huge hit with the kiddos!

- If you do not have a cheese wedge, you can use a gym mat placed on its edge, which works the same way.

3. Wax Museum/Toy Story

Equipment Needed

- None

Set-Up

Have all children stand with both feet on the end line facing the instructor.

The instructor will stand on the other end of the gym.

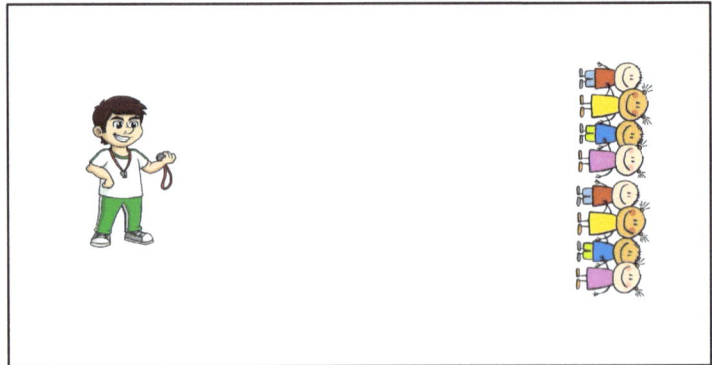

Instructions

1. Explain to the children they are Andy's toys from *Toy Story* and ask them to pick a character, which makes it even more fun for them and you. As the instructor, you will be Andy, and they are currently in his bedroom.
2. When the instructor/Andy faces the children, they must be frozen in any pose of their choosing.
3. When you turn around, also known as leave the room, the children/Andy's Toys may quietly tiptoe close to the instructor.
4. When the instructor turns around and faces the children, they must freeze wherever they are standing.
5. At this point, the instructor walks around pretending to be confused at how the toys have moved. To keep the children engaged, point out some cool poses the children made.
6. If a child moves, the instructor should ask them to go back to the beginning or as a variation, take a few steps backward.
7. Repeat this process a few times until they get closer to the instructor.

On the last turn, stay with your back to the children, so they get really close to you, and when you turn, say, "Wait, my toys are alive," and chase them back to the line and try to tag them before they get there.

Variation

- Instead of the instructor being Andy and the children his toys, the instructor can be the museum curator and the children can be wax statues. When facing the children the instructor yells, "Wax museum open," the children must freeze in place, and when the instructor says, "Wax museum closed," the instructor turns their back to the children. At that point, the children tiptoe forward until the museum is open. Repeat the process several times.

4. Parachute Games – Shake the Coach

Equipment Needed

- 1 sport's parachute
- 4-6 Softballs or small beach balls

Set-Up

Lay the parachute out flat in the center of the playing area.

One at a time, ask the children to find a spot on the parachute to sit. Please note they should have their legs beneath the parachute and should hold on to the side of it with two hands and magnetize those hands to their knees.

The instructor should join them in the circle and find their own space with their legs beneath the parachute too.

Instructions

1. You will build up to the Shake the Coach game. First play red light green light parachute style – red freeze, yellow shake slow, green shake fast, and blue is for take a nap.
2. Go around the circle and give each child a chance to pick a light color and everyone has to follow those instructions. Be warned; they love the taking a nap light!
3. After everyone has had a turn, ask the children to stand and go get four to six softballs to put in the parachute. Be sure they do not shake it until instructed. They need to follow instructions. When the instructor says, "Go," see how many seconds it takes for them to shake all the balls out of the parachute. Make sure you let them know not to go after the balls that have fallen out. When all balls are out, be sure to be excited about their accomplishment and ask them if they think during the next round, they can do it even faster. Children love challenges.
4. After another round, ask them to sit down as they will now be playing Shake the Coach.
5. Now, the instructor goes into the center of the parachute with the balls inside. Create a story that you snuck into the classroom last night and tried to steal their lunches, the balls, but they catch you. They will need to shake the parachute as the instructor runs around it, trying to catch as many balls as they can. Fall a few times as that will get big laughs. Of course, by the end of the round, you don't steal any of the balls to keep them engaged in the activity.
6. Next, all that running around has made the instructor tired; so, lay down in the parachute. Tell the children they can only shake the parachute when you fall asleep and snores. When you are awake, the children must not shake the parachute. When the instructor falls asleep and starts to snore, the children can shake the parachute and wake you up. You should act surprised and say, "Hey, how did I end up here?" and then fall back asleep. At that time, the children will again shake the parachute to wake you up. Repeat a few times!

5. Fox in the Hen House

Equipment Needed

- 1 soccer ball per child

Set-Up

Give each child one soccer ball.

Ask them to find a spot in the designated play area and put one foot on the ball.

Instructions

1. Children should be spread out in the play area with their foot on top of the ball.
2. The children are the hens, and the ball is their egg. The instructor is the fox.
3. When the instructor says, "Dribble," the children can freely dribble the ball around the play area.
4. When the instructor yells, "Fox in the hen house," they must hide their soccer ball (egg) by sitting on it before the fox eats it.
5. The instructor should go around acting confused at where the eggs went and look everywhere for them. Ask, "Hey, do you have an egg?" Most will reply, "No!"
6. Repeat for a few rounds. If you do happen to take an egg, put it inside your shirt like you ate it, and then make sure the child whose egg you took politely asks for it back.

Variations

- Can be done with basketballs.

6. Ant Tag

Equipment Needed

- 4 pinnies – sports shirts
- 6 poly spots or cones

Set-Up

Have all children start at one end of the playing area.

Pick two or four children to be the exterminators, give each a pinnie, and have them start on the opposite end of the playing area.

Place five poly sports or cones around the playing area, which will be the hospitals. Poly spots work better because children cannot kick them down when playing.

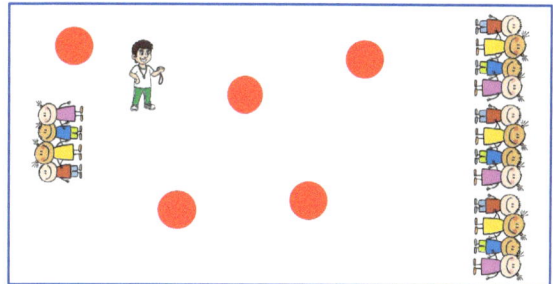

Instructions

1. Have all children line up on one end of the play area; they will be the ants.
2. Pick two or four children to be the exterminators, have them put on the pinnie and have them start on the other side of the playing area.
3. Say, "Go!" When you do, the ants run around the playing area and try not to get tagged by the exterminators.
4. If an ant gets tagged by an exterminator, they must freeze where they are, lay on their back, and put their hands and legs in the air as they are now a sick ant.
5. Any time a child gets tagged, the instructor who will be the ambulance, runs over to the sick ant, grabs their ankles, and pulls them to one of the poly spots, which is the hospital where they get better. Go back into the game and start the chase again. Trust me, this may sound violent, but the children love the ride to the hospital! You will defiantly get an excellent work out saving all the sick ants in this game.
6. Each round should last no more than a minute.
7. After each round, pick two to four new exterminators.
8. Those that were exterminators are now ants.

Variation

- The same game can be played with cones.

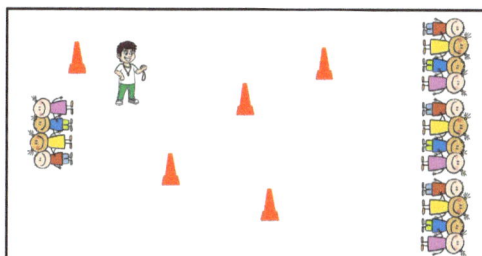

7. Jailbreak

Equipment Needed

- 4 pinnies (sport's game shirts)
- 8 cones

Set-Up

Have all children start at one end of the play area.

Pick two or four children to be the police. They will start on the opposite end of the playing area and have a pinnie on or police badge if you have any.

Place eight cones around in a rectangle in one corner of the play area; this will be the jail.

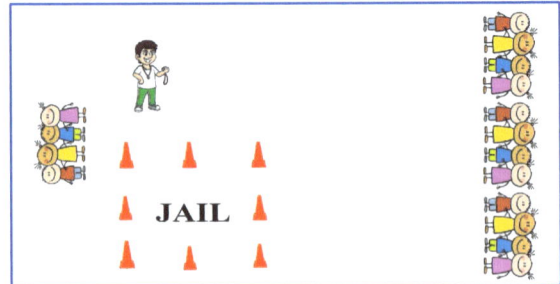

Instructions

1. Have all children lined up on one end of the play area they will be the burglars.
2. Pick two to four children to be the police, have them put on the pinnie and have them start on the other side of the play area.
3. The instructor should tell a story about the burglars taking all the money from the bank (or any other age-appropriate story) and that the police are trying to tag them.
4. On go, the children will run around the play area trying to avoid being tagged by the police.
5. If a burglar gets tagged by the police, the police will hold hands with that child and escort them to the jail area.
6. To get out of the jail, another child must run into the jail and give them a high five, and then they are back in the game.
7. Each round should last no more than a minute.
8. After each round, pick two to four new police.
9. Those that were the police are now burglars.

Variations

- Instead of going to jail when they are tagged, they can freeze where they got tagged and need to get a high five from a friend to get back in the game.

8. Gaga

Equipment Needed

- 1-5 soft dodge balls

Set-Up

Have the children circle the instructor.

The instructor should start either holding one soft dodge ball or place one to five soft dodge balls at various places.

Instructions

1. The instructor holds the ball while the children are in a circle around.
2. The instructor bounces the ball three times while saying, "Ga." Each time they bounce it to start the game.
3. On the third bounce, the children can break off from the circle and run wherever they like within the boundary area.
4. The instructor is the only one that can touch the ball at this time.
5. Using one hand, the instructor goes around trying to knock the ball into the children. If a ball hits a child below the knees, they must freeze and can get a high-five from another child to get back in the game.
6. Each round should last one or two minutes.
7. Each next round starts with the instructor holding the ball in the middle with children circled up around them.
8. Each round you can add more balls, and if more than one instructor you can have them try to get the children too.

Variations

- Starting the same way, with the instructor in middle and children in a circle around them, grab five balls. On "Go!" it's everyone for themselves. Anyone can try to hit the ball into another player using only one hand. Just like before, if a child gets hit by the ball below the knees, they are frozen, and anyone can give them a high-five to get you back into the game; including the person that hit them.

- Instead of getting frozen, when a child gets out, instruct them to sit down. When the ball goes to them, they can use their hands to hit the ball into someone's legs. If they succeed, they are back in the game.

9. Messy Yard

Equipment Needed

- 20 to 30 ball pit balls
- 8 cones or a tennis net
- Music player (optional)

Set-Up

Divide the boundary in half with cones or a tennis net.

Have all children on one side and instructor on the other.

Place all the balls on the side where the children are. They should not touch the balls until instructed.

The instructor tells a story that you are their new neighbor, and on your side of the fence is your yard and on their side is theirs. Then late at night, you dump all your trash (the balls) into their yard.

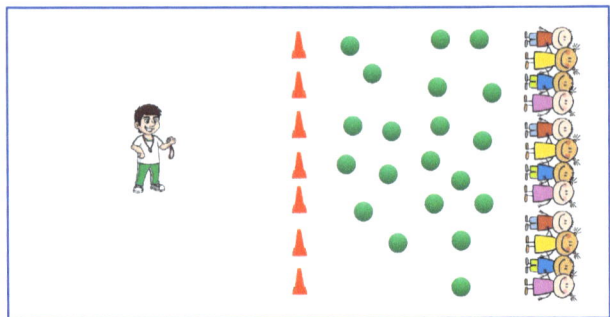

Instructions

1. Ask the children to pick up one ball and inform them that they can only hold one ball at a time.
2. On "Go!" they must clean their yard by throwing the balls into the instructor's yard. As they are throwing their trash into the instructor's yard, the instructor will try to throw the trash back into the children's yard.
3. After two minutes, the instructor should count down from five to zero. Once they get to zero, everyone must run back to the boundary line.
4. The instructor will walk over to the children on their side of the yard, and say, "Wow, your yard looks so clean. I better not turn around and see all your trash in my yard."
5. The instructor will then turn around and act surprised to see all the trash in his yard. The children will get a good laugh out of it.
6. Now the side of the yard with all the balls in it is their yard for the next round, and the instructor will be on the other side.
7. Play two or three rounds.
8. Make a game out of picking up all the balls and see how fast they can clean them all up.

Variations

- If children are older, you can divide them into two groups and have a group on each side of the fence.

- Instead of keeping time, the game can start when the music starts and when the music stops, children must drop any ball and sit down wherever they are.

10. Magic Paper Run/Snowball Fight

Equipment Needed

- 1 sheet of paper per child

Set-Up

The children should be sitting down at one end of the boundary.

The instructor hands each child a magic sheet of paper and tells them they cannot let it touch the ground, or it will lose its magic.

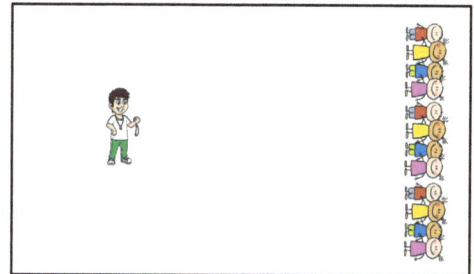

Instructions

1. The instructor asks all children to stand and line up with both feet on the end boundary.

2. The instructor will demonstrate by taking the magic paper and holding it up against their chest, long ways like a hot dog. Then the instructor will start running while holding the paper than will lift their hands up. Keep running, and the paper will magically stick to the instructor while they do.

3. Next, the children will try, and on "Go!" they will start to run holding the paper long ways against their chest. When the instructor says, "Lift your hands up and keep running," all children will run, and to their surprise, the paper will stick to them like magic!

4. Repeat one more time, then have the children sit.

5. Once they sit, have children use their strong muscles to turn the sheet of paper into a ball.

6. Once every child has used their magical muscles to turn the paper into a snowball, the instructor will now have a fun and safe snowball fight.

7. Children will then stand holding their snowball and on "Go!" will chase the instructor and try to throw the snowball and hit the instructor. This is a fun way to work on throwing, and it does not hurt to get hit by the paper ball, so it is safe as well!

Variations

- Before having the snowball fight, the instructor can give the children a few minutes to throw the snowball around the playing area so they can practice their throwing.

11. The Magic Cones

Equipment Needed

- 15-20 cones
- 1 tennis ball per child

Set-Up

Find a chain-link fence. Usually, a baseball field backstop and dugout fence work perfectly for this activity.

Place cones into the fence by placing the top of the cone through the holes until it stays.

Have each child hold a tennis ball and line up shoulder to shoulder about five yards from the fence.

Instructions

1. The object of the game is for the children to throw the cones and try to knock them off the fence.
2. The instructor should make sure everyone stands shoulder to shoulder and then yell, "Throw!" to instruct the children that it is time to throw the balls at the cones. There is an exceedingly high probability that many of the cones will fall off, giving them confidence.
3. Make sure no one goes after their ball until the instructor lets them know it is safe to do so.
4. Continue for a few more rounds until all cones are knocked off the fence.

Variations

- Time the group to see how long it takes them to knock all the cones off the fence.

- Have them go one at a time and have them cheer on their classmates.

- When you are setting the game up, sometimes the cones you already put into the fence fall off. If that happens, face the kids, and say, "Hey, who used their magic powers to knock that cone off the fence." They will get a kick out of it!

12. Jump the Snake

Equipment Needed

- 1 long jump rope
- Tape or a heavy object
- 1 poly spot

Set-Up

Children will be seated on one end of the boundary in a line.

Rope will be laid out ten yards in front of children.

The instructor will tape or anchor one end of the rope down and hold the other end.

The instructor will tell a story of how they led the class into the jungle, but took a wrong turn, got lost, and a snake is in their way that they will need to jump over to get to safety.

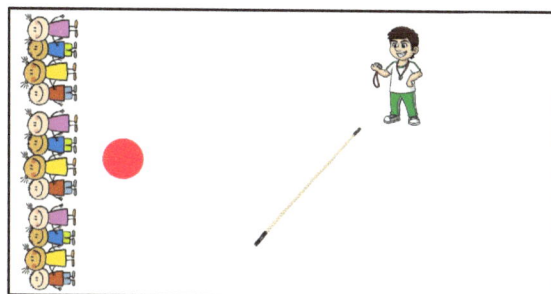

Instructions

1. One at a time, the instructor will call up a child and have them stand on the poly spot.
2. On "Go!" the child will walk up to the snake, position both feet on the ground, bend their knees, place their arms behind them, and jump over the snake. When they do, they must sit on the other side of the snake about five yards from it to give the other children plenty of room to jump.
3. Each child will then get a turn to jump over the snake.
4. Now that the children are on the other side of the snake, they will now need to jump back over; but this time the snake has awoken and is very angry so the instructor will shake the snake to make it harder and more fun to jump over.
5. Again, each child will get a turn to jump over the snake, but if the snake touches them when they jump over, they will need to drink the magic potion that only the instructor is holding. So, they will run over to the instructor, grab the magical potion, and drink it, so they don't get sick.
6. Can do two to three rounds.

Variations

- Have the children jump over with a partner.

- Have all the children jump over at the same time; they don't run over, they tiptoe quietly up to the snake so they don't wake him and then at the same time will jump over the snake.

- On the final round, have all the children line up next to the snake and instead of jumping over, have them jump up and down on it, which is a fun way to end the game.

13. Knock the Hat Off

Equipment Needed

- 1 Hat

Set-Up

Have the children either sit in a circle around the instructor or form a line.

The instructor wears a hat.

This simple game will help you get the attention of the children; and at the very end, have them quiet and ready to listen.

Instructions

1. Tell the children that when the hat is on your head, they must be absolutely quiet.
2. Then tell them when the hat is off your head, they can scream and yell and get all their sillies out.
3. Take the hat off your head or even better pretend your hat accidentally got knocked off and the children will start to yell.
4. Quickly place the hat back on your head and see how they quiet down.
5. Repeat a few times.
6. The last time when you place the hat on your head, they will quickly get quiet, and you will be able to transition them into the next activity or area you want them to go next.

Variations

- If you don't have a hat, a cone works just as well.

14. Builders & Bulldozers

Equipment Needed

- 15-20 comes

Set-Up

Set up the cones around the playing area standing up. They should be evenly spread out throughout the playing area.

Children start the game standing on one end of the boundaries.

Instructions

1. The instructor will be the builder. All cones are the instructor's houses that he has built on the children's land.
2. The children are the bulldozers. On "Go!" the children run around the playing area knocking the cones down with their hands (no feet).
3. As the children knock the cones down, the builder will run around trying to set them back upright.
4. When the instructor says, "Stop!" all children need to stop knocking down cones and run back to an area designated by the instructor.
5. In the next round, you can either have the same rules; or you can split the children up where half will be builders and the other half bulldozers. If you choose to do that, play two rounds, so each child has a chance to be a builder and a bulldozer.

Variations

- Less of a variation, and more of a fun way to have the children clean up after the game. Since there will be cones everywhere, the instructor should sit down with legs stretched out and shoes pointed to the sky. Ask the children to go around and pick up the cones. Inform them that they can only pick up one at a time, and then they must bring it over to the instructor where they can place the cone over one of the instructor's shoes or over one of the instructor's hands. They can also choose to give the instructor a hat and place it on their head. The children will have fun giving the instructor a new outfit, and before you know it, everything will be cleaned up, and the children will be sitting in front of you.

The Best Songs for Early Childhood Gym

♫

Why are these the best Songs for early childhood gym, you ask? Not only are these songs great to listen to, but they are also called listen and follow direction songs, which means the songs will engage the children. As they listen to the songs, they can perform the movements that it asks. The songs are all great warm-ups to an early childhood gym class or if you just want your child to burn off some energy in a structured environment. There is one exception, and that is *Raffi's Baby Beluga*, because it is not a listen and follow direction song, it simply was my favorite song when I was in preschool!

Songs

- *Self-Control* (Toddler Version) by David Kisor
- *Jim Along Josie* by Parachute Express
- *Stand Up, Sit Down* by Tumble Tots
- *Reach up High* by Parachute Express
- *Pass the Bean Bag* by Tumble Tots
- *I Can Run as Fast as You* by Tumble Tots
- *Shake my Sillies* by Tumble Tots
- *Hot Potato* by The Wiggles
- *Up Down Turn Around* by Tumble Tots
- *Put Your Finger on* by Parachute Express
- *Shake Break* by Pancake Manor
- *Listen and Move* by Unknown
- *I'm Gonna Catch You* by Laurie Berkner Band
- *Baby Beluga* by Raffi

Note: Songs can be found on my Spotify Playlist titled "28 Best Games & Songs for Early Childhood Gym."

28 Best Tips, Tricks, and Things to Remember when Teaching Early Childhood

1. You Must Have High Energy and Charisma – The energy you have during the games will match the energy of the children. If you teach with low energy, the children will not be as engaged and will have way less fun than if you are high energy and energetic!

2. Your Early Childhood Gym Class Should be Structured – It is great to start your class with everyone sitting in a circle. That way you can go over the rules, have an opening song, a warm-up song, two or three fun, and engaging activities, and then end again in a circle. It is important to have quick a debrief and fun goodbye song; and if you keep that structure for each class, the children will know what to expect, and in turn, will have more fun and will behave better.

3. Have Fun - You should have as much fun if not more fun than the children you are working with in your program.

4. Be Goofy - Do not be afraid to act goofy or silly while teaching early childhood classes.

5. Add Humor - Use humor throughout to keep children engaged.

6. Keep Children Engaged - It is important to keep the children engaged, especially during transitions. It would help if you always were talking with them even when you are setting up your next game. For example, if the game calls for a lot of cones to be set up around the play area, instead of quietly putting the cones out, engage the children by asking them where you should toss the next cone. You can toss the cones one at a time high in the air, and the children will be mesmerized in how high you are throwing them, which will keep them engaged. By the time you throw the last cone, you will be all set up for the game and the children will still be where you left them sitting nicely awaiting your instruction. Alternatively, you can give each child a cone and use it to help you set up the game.

7. Sing a Happy Tune - Don't just simply tell the kids to go stand against the wall or make a circle, have a simple song with a familiar tune that they sing each time. They will get used to it, which will keep them more engaged than simply pointing and telling them where to go.

8. Plan the Activity - Be prepared, not only should you be prepared with a lesson plan you should also have contingency plans, and extra games up your sleeve in case a game or activity does not go as long as you anticipated.

9. Know What Activity Works for Each Age Group - Just because a game or activity did not work out with one age group, does not mean it won't work with other groups. There has been plenty of times where a group of children the same age and I will have one group love the game we laid while the other just did not understand it or were not into it and that is totally okay.

10. Tweak the Game - If a game or activity you try does not work out do not give up on it. Figure out how you can tweak it to make it better.

11. Create Variations - The games and activities I play are always evolving. What is even better, I got a lot of ideas for improving my games and activities from how the children interpret the game. Many of the best variations to my games are from things the children did while playing the games, which is absolutely awesome.

12. Stop Game in Time - End the game or activity when the children are having the most fun. Do not try to stretch the game out because the children are enjoying it because that is when you will have the game go on too long and the fun will end. Problems will start when a game is extended, and then the lasting memory of the activity for the child will not be a good one.

13. Involve Others - If you are working with other teachers, get them involved. All teachers and instructors should be either leading the activity or participating in it. Children will see the adults having fun playing and will be more likely to engage in the activity as well.

14. Focus Your Attention on the Children Who Play - If a child does not want to play, they can sit it out, but there is no reason for a teacher or instructor to sit with them and give them attention. Attention should be given to the children who are participating, and eventually, that child who is sitting out will want to join in. if the teacher or instructor sits with the child who does not want to play, it encourages other children to do the same even if they want to play.

15. Be Creative - Go the extra mile, a lot of times a game or activity can be made better because you put in the extra effort and were creative. For instance, when making giant life-size cut-outs of a baseball catcher, laminating them, and then cutting a hole in the mitt for the children to have fun with a bean bag toss, instead of just having them throw into the bucket.

16. Go Big - Giant anything will get their attention; whether it be giant dice or a soccer ball three times bigger than their heads. The items that you can use in games and activities that bring a wow factor will always keep the children engaged.

17. Read Books to Enhance Activities - Using books in gym class is another fantastic way to keep them engaged. I once read the book, "There Was an Old Lady Who Swallowed a Fly," and after each animal she ate, the children had to go around the designated area pretending to be that animal.

18. Learn from Each Lesson - There will be days where your class did not go how you wanted it to go, and that is okay. It does not mean you are not a good teacher. Though you should learn from it and use what you learn to improve yourself as a teacher/instructor.

19. Bubbles to the Rescue - Do you want to keep children engaged during an activity or game, use bubbles? The children can chase and pop them all day. I recommend buying a few bubble wands that allow you to be mobile and crank out thousands of bubbles at a time.

20. Reinforce Good Behavior - Stickers or stamps are great to give out at the end of class. It gives the children something to look forward to and will help overall behavior throughout as well.

21. High-Fives - High-fives are the best; children love getting high-fives, but remember if you give out one, you're going to have to give out one to the rest of the group. No matter how hard the high-five, you must pretend like it was the hardest high-five you have ever received.

22. Be Consistent in Disciplinary Actions - You must follow through on your disciplinary actions. If you let the children know they will have to take a break if they are exhibiting inappropriate behavior, you must follow through and have them sit out. There is no giving first, second, or third warnings because that will show the class that they can get away with poor behavior.

23. Remember Children Forget - No matter how upset a child seems to be with you at a given moment, they will always forget why they were upset with you and will give you the biggest hug that makes your day.

24. Give it Your All - You owe it to every child to give it your best every day. In return, they will give you theirs; most the time! ☺

25. Converse With the Children - Engage children in conversation, whether you tell them that I love their shirt, ask them what they had for breakfast or by telling them how cool their shoes are, it is important to converse with them.

26. Poly Spots Make Your Job Easier - Invest in poly spots; they make giving directions a lot easier.

27. Provide Opportunities for Free Play - Free play is just as important as structured play. Free play gives a child the chance to explore, be creative, and interact with other children.

28. Give Children Winning Opportunities - Let them win, most the time. I know it's important to teach how to be a good loser, but letting them win will boost their confidence and keep tears to a minimum. I race with the children every day in my gym classes, and I have still been unable to beat them. However, I always have a smile on my face despite my last place finish. ☺

THE END... For now!

About the Author

Cameron Edelman, Hey that's me! I am a graduate of Illinois State University, where I received a degree in Recreation Management. I have spent the past seven years working in the recreation field as a sports manager/Gym teacher at a non-profit community center, and currently; I am a Recreation Supervisor for a park district. A considerable part of my job these past years has been creating early childhood gym curriculum for preschool gym and sports programs as well as instructing amazingly fun and engaging classes. I also have a background in summer camps, so not only are the children learning so much in my gym classes, but they are having loads of fun, and there are tons of laughs and smiles too. Teaching and building creative and inventive early childhood gym and sports curriculum is my real passion, and I am so lucky to be doing something I love and glad I can share the knowledge I have with you in this book.